AF428393

DID THE WORLD WAR II SPIES HAVE SUPER COOL GADGETS?

History Book about Wars
Children's Military Books

All sides in World War II used spies to try to find out what their enemies were planning and doing. Some spies used gadgets that were pretty cool for their day, even if they were nothing like what the latest James Bond has! Let's take a look.

SPIES AT WORK

In a war, spies have a wide range of jobs:

↳ They try to find out what the enemy is planning, and where enemy troops are, and then get that information back to their own side.

↳ They try to "turn" enemy soldiers or politicians so they provide information the spy could not otherwise get.

↳ They may try to disrupt what the enemy is doing, using everything from explosives to sugar in gas tanks.

↳ In their home country, they try to track down the enemy's spies and stop their work, or even "turn" the spies into double agents.

The best spies did not look like super-heroes or people you see in magazines. They tried to look like everyday, inoffensive people who could blend right in wherever they were.

Spies had the best chance of succeeding when anybody who saw them would dismiss them as a risk or as something out of place. That man on the bicycle? Oh, he is just a delivery boy for the butcher or the baker.

The person being spied on might never find out that secret information had been stolen and passed along to the other side, sometimes by that innocent-looking guy who just went by on the delivery bicycle!

World War II officially started in 1939 and ran until Germany and Japan surrendered to the Allies in 1945. However, spies were hard at work for years before the start of the war, to help their countries prepare for what might come. Here are some of the tools they worked with.

WORLD WAR II

SECRET WEAPONS

Lots of spy weapons were concealed as other things so nobody would think twice about them. Other weapons were very small, or hidden in unusual places.

ESCAPE KNIFE

This was the parent to the multi-tools of today, that often have a hammer, a small saw, and several screwdrivers all attached to a single handle.

MULTI TOOLS

The spy version in WWII had three small saw blades for cutting wood and metal, a blade for cutting or punching holes in car tires, and a wire cutter. The tools all folded into a single handle, and the whole thing could be slipped into a pocket.

AN IRON KEY

In World War II many houses had locks that required large, elaborate keys. A spy might have a big key on his key ring that didn't fit any door. However, if you unscrewed the head off the key, you could find a secret compartment. There you could carry a document, a map, poison pills, or some other essential for your work.

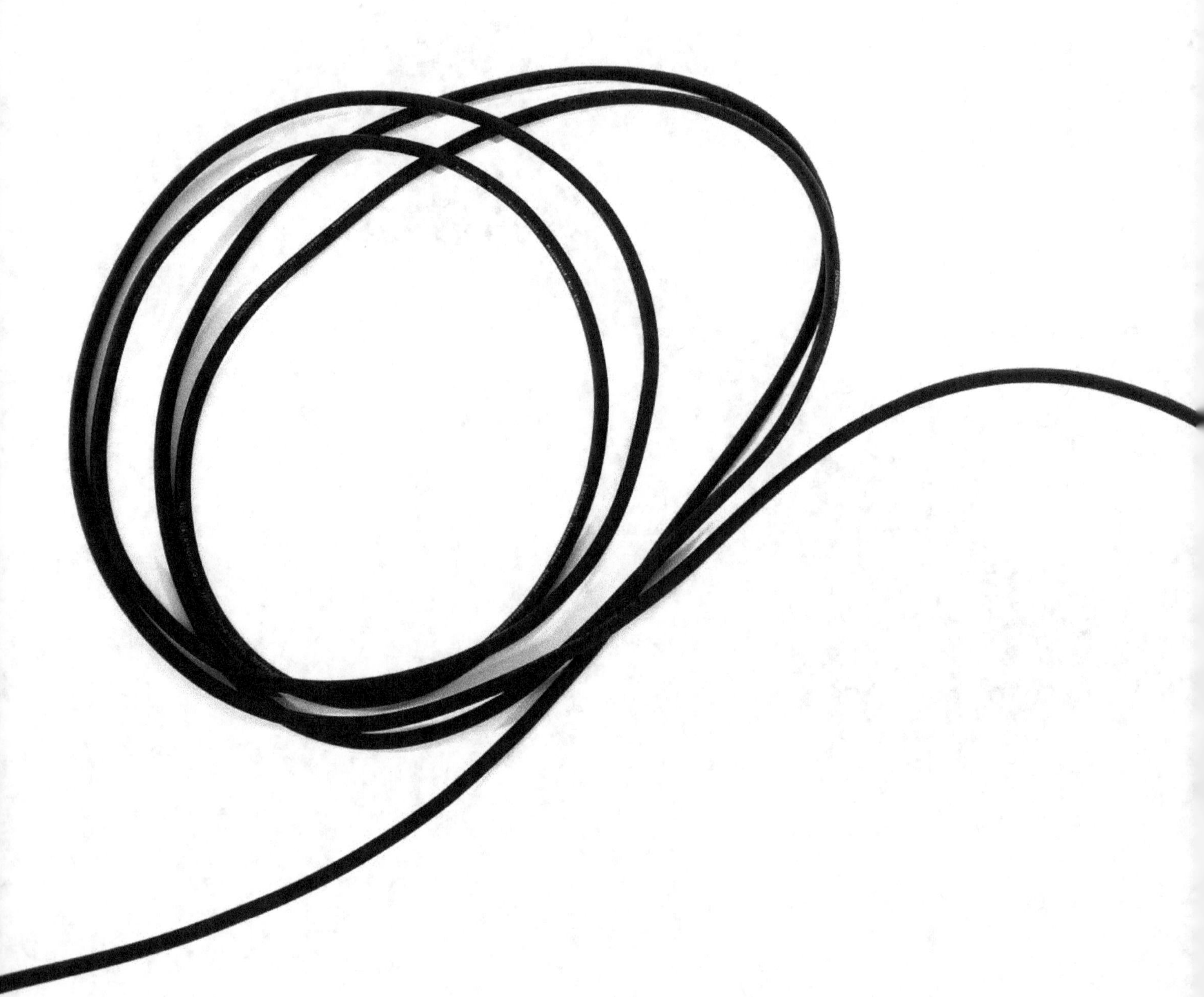

GARROTTE

A wire with loops at each end does not look like much. But stick a bit of wood through each loop to use as a handle, and you have a weapon with which you could attack and choke a sentry or an enemy spy. Then you could throw the handles away in one place, and the wire in another place, and get rid of the evidence of the attack.

DANGEROUS PEN

A pen, that might have been a gift from a rich uncle, will even write if you have to show it is really a pen. But if you open it in a special way, it reveals a sharp stabbing blade.

DECORATIVE PIN

Many people in the 1930s and 1940s wore decorative pins on the lapels of their coats. The pin might have the emblem of a hiking club, or some national symbol like a German eagle. Real pins like this were no longer than was required to attach to the coat; but a spy might wear such a pin at the head of a long dagger. The rest of the dagger would be hidden in the collar of the coat, ready to appear when the spy needed it.

LIBERATOR PISTOL

The Liberator was a single-shot pistol that was only accurate over short range, but it fired a 45-caliber bullet that was very effective if it hit its target. It was cheap and easy to make, and because it was so small it was easy for a spy to hide one until he needed to use it.

BLACK JOE

Coal grenades were first invented during the American Civil War, 1861-65. They are explosives disguised to look like lumps of coal. The spy or saboteur would drop some into the coal bin of a furnace, or a train or ship engine.

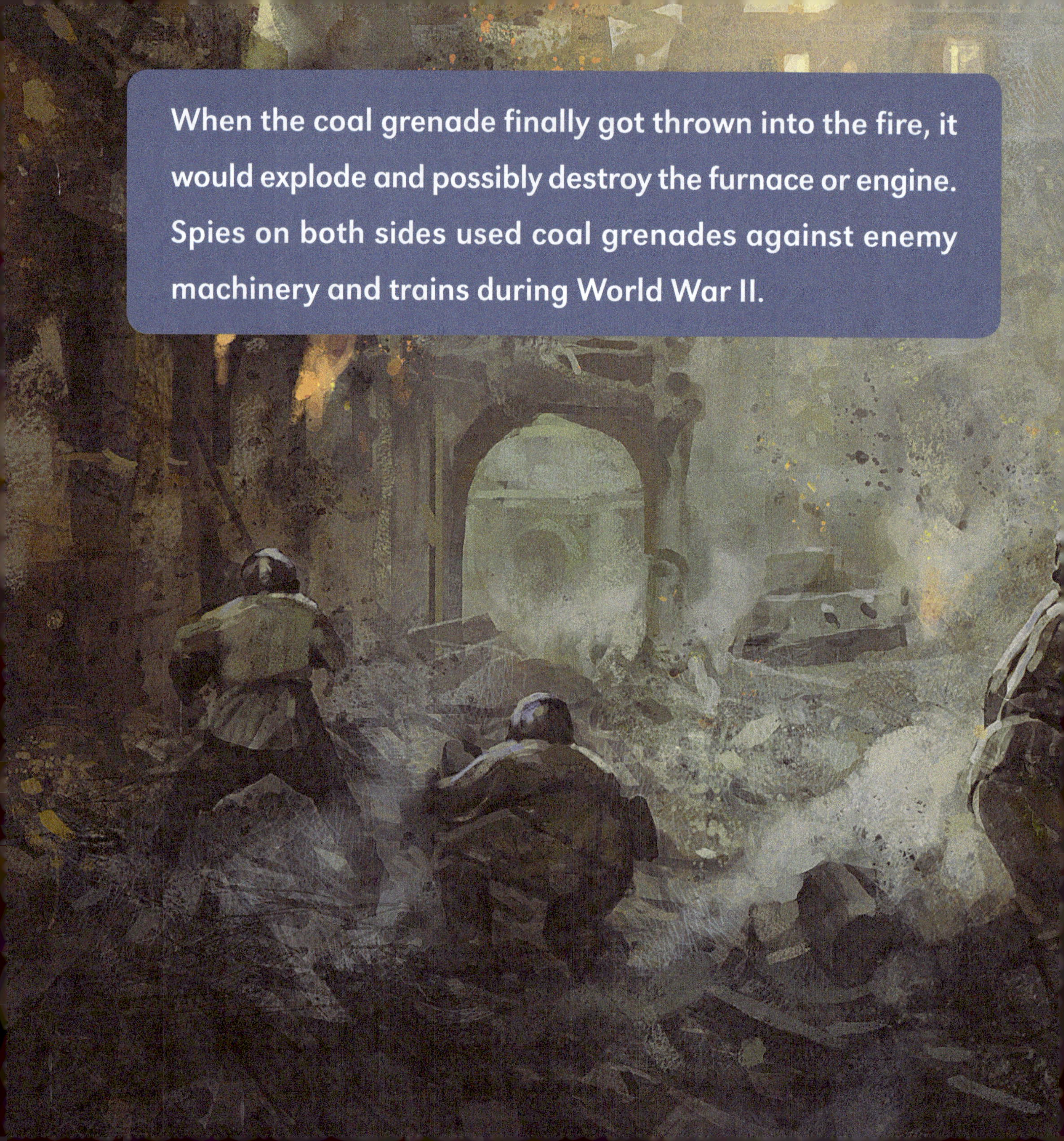

When the coal grenade finally got thrown into the fire, it would explode and possibly destroy the furnace or engine. Spies on both sides used coal grenades against enemy machinery and trains during World War II.

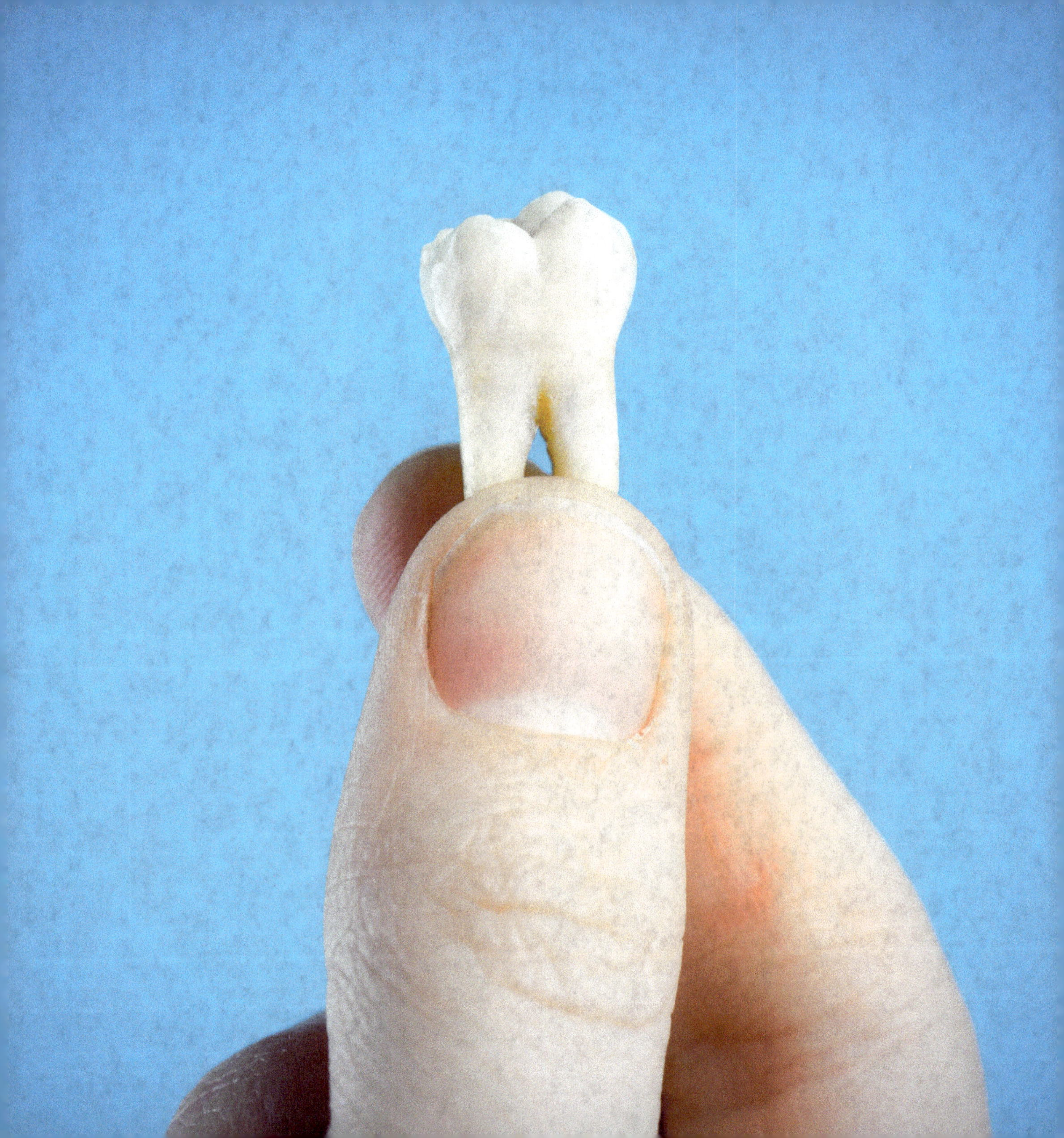

POISON TOOTH

One of the worst things for a spy is to be captured—not just because things will go badly for the spy, but because under torture the spy may reveal information that harms his own side. Many spies carried with them poison of some sort that they could take if they were going to be captured. This would not save their lives, but it might save the lives of others on their side. Sometimes this poison was concealed inside a hollow false tooth in the spy's mouth.

GETTING AND SHARING INFORMATION

Spies knew they might not get back alive from their missions, but that their information had to get back—and the quicker the better! So they had a number of ways of staying in touch.

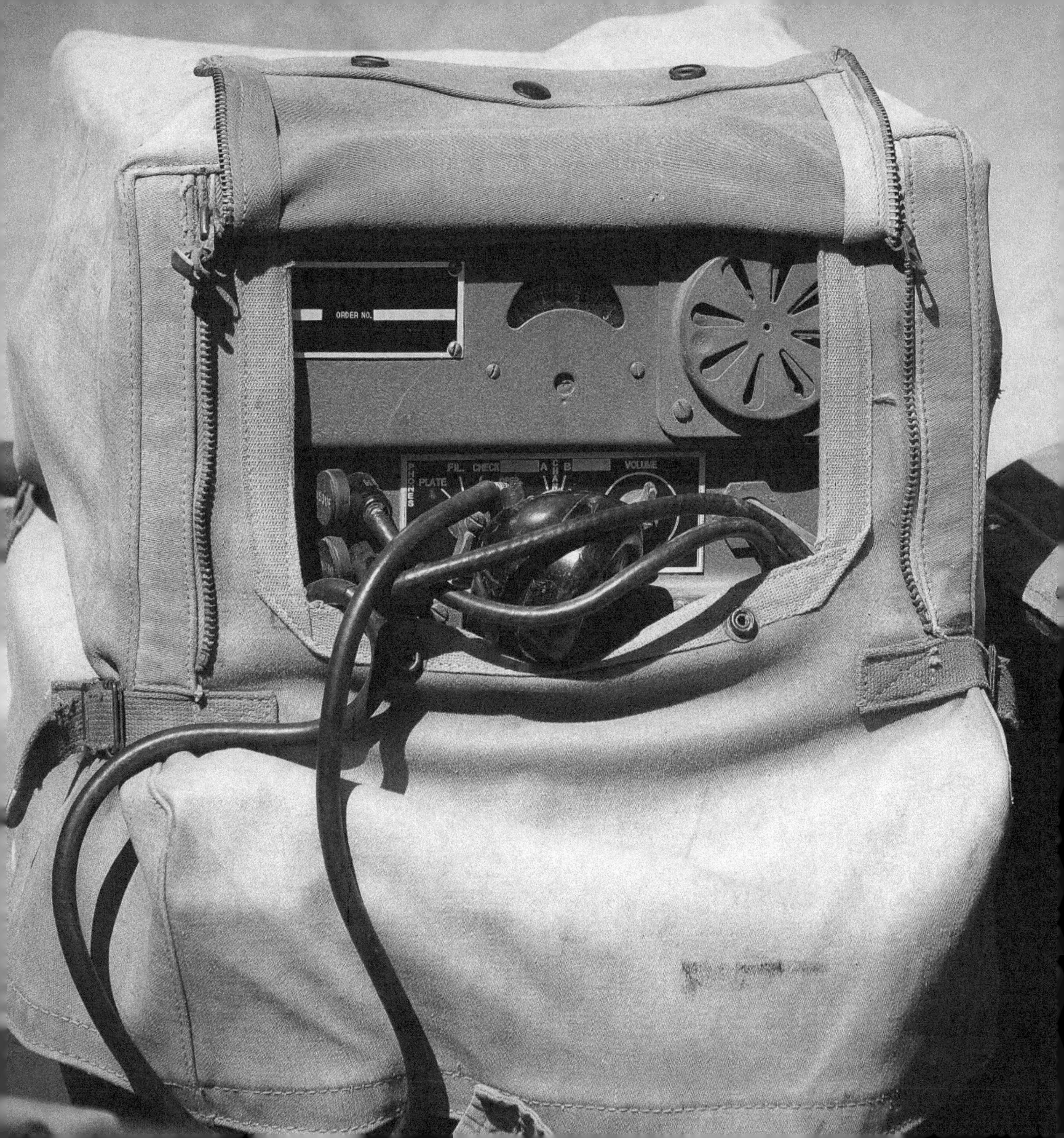

ORDER NO.
PHONES
PLATE
FIL. CHECK
A C B
VOLUME

H/L LOCK
OFF SQL-O-VOL   DIAL
CODE
POWER CHARGE TRICKLE
QUICK CHARGER

THE J-E

The Joan-Eleanor System was a high-frequency radio. The spy had a transmitter-receiver, and a similar unit would be on a plane. If the plane flew low over where the spy was, the two units could communicate. It was almost impossible for the enemy to intercept these conversations, or even know they were happening, but it was very risky for the crew of the airplanes. This system was considered so valuable that it remained a secret until 1976, long after the war was over.

BISCUIT TIN RADIO

Other British spies carried radios so compact they would fit in a biscuit tin or a suitcase. The spy would set up the radio at an agreed time in the day and listen for messages sent from London. They could also transmit short messages in code, but this was very risky.

PAŃSTWOWE ZAKŁADY TELE-RADJOTECHNICZN WARSZAWA
Nr
Nr 813
REGUL.
RĘCZNY
AUTO
TELEFON TELEGRAF ZESTAW
FALA ODB.
DOSTROJENIE FALA ZAKRES
ZASILANIE
SŁUCHAWK.
A-NAD
A-ODB
A-NAD
A-ODB
FALA NADAW.
UWAGA
PAŃSTWOWE ZAKŁADY TELE-RADJOTECHNICZN WARSZAWA
Nr
Nr 813
TELEFON TELEGRAF
MIKROTELE
MIKROFON
KLUCZ
ZASILANIE
ZAKRES

The Germans had very good devices for locating radio transmissions, and the spy would have to finish the transmission quickly and leave the scene within minutes to avoid getting caught.

PEDAL POWER

Spies sometimes carried with them a generator they could attach to the wheel of a bicycle. When they peddled the bike, the generator would charge the batteries in the spy's radio or other equipment.

SINGLE-USE CODES

Some spies carried little pads of paper, or small books that looked like novels or collections of poetry. But if you knew where to look, you could find on each page different rules for encoding a message. If you sent what page you used at the start of the message, your colleague who received the message would know how to decode it. Then you would destroy the page off the pad, or never use that page in the book again.

FINDING YOUR WAY

Spies, as well as escaping prisoners of war, had to know how to get to where they needed to go. Agencies provided clever ways to provide maps and other aids to navigation.

300
280
260
240
220
W
NW
SW
S
SE
E
NE
20
40
60
80
100
120
Black
bog
Bay

PLAYING CARD MAPS

Spy agencies developed decks of playing cards that looked perfectly normal. But one or more cards could be peeled apart to show a map on the inside of the two halves of the card. This might be essential for a spy who did not want to draw attention by asking too many questions.

BUTTON COMPASSES

Many spies and even regular-duty officers had special buttons on their coats or uniform jackets. The buttons could unscrew to reveal a compass you could use to figure out where north was and therefore where you should go next.

PASSEPORT
25K
25K
1210.42
10.42
Pont
Villa
lon

FALSE DOCUMENTS

Whenever possible, spies carried identification papers, ration cards, travel documents, and other material that looked just as good as the real documents the enemy country provided. It was a constant struggle to keep up with documents, as of course governments and agencies changed them regularly. Whole departments worked at getting examples of the latest documents and then generating accurate fakes that agents could use with confidence.

THE BEST EQUIPMENT

Beyond all this stuff, the very best spies brought these skills to their work: the ability to observe, and to remember what they saw; acting skill, so they could be someone they were not; a gift for languages; and cool heads at tense moments, so they could do what had to be done even when they might be arrested or shot at any moment.

Do you have those skills? Perhaps spycraft lies in your future!

Read more about the times in which WWII spies operated in Baby Professor books like The Brave Women of World War II, The Allied Powers vs. the Axis Powers in World War II, and The Theaters of World War II: Europe and the Pacific.

Visit
BABY PROFESSOR
EDUCATION KIDS
www.BabyProfessorBooks.com
to download Free Baby Professor eBooks
and view our catalog of new and exciting
Children's Books